WATERSPOUTS

Marne Ventura

childsworld.com

Published by The Child's World®
800-599-READ • www.childsworld.com

Copyright © 2025 by The Child's World®
All rights reserved. No part of this book may be reproduced or utilized in any form or by any means without written permission from the publisher.

Photography Credits
Photographs ©: Antonio S./Shutterstock Images, cover, 1; Shutterstock Images, 2–3; Lt. Jeff Shoup/NOAA, 5; iStockphoto, 6; lunzhakova Iuliia/Shutterstock Images, 8; Milan Noga/Shutterstock Images, 9; Jeff Gammons/Shutterstock Images, 11; Dr. Joseph Golden/NOAA, 13 (top), 13 (bottom); Bobby Kent/Shutterstock Images, 14 (left); Philip Thurston/iStockphoto, 14 (right); Kevin Poirier/The Kenosha News/AP Images, 17; Rob Atherton/Shutterstock Images, 18; Minerva Studio/Shutterstock Images, 21

ISBN Information
9781503894440 (Reinforced Library Binding)
9781503895201 (Portable Document Format)
9781503896024 (Online Multi-user eBook)
9781503896840 (Electronic Publication)

LCCN 2024942898

Printed in the United States of America

ABOUT THE AUTHOR
Marne Ventura is the author of more than 150 books for children. She holds a master's degree in education from the University of California. She enjoys writing about STEM, arts and crafts, finance, people and places, food, and careers. Ventura and her family live in California.

CONTENTS

CHAPTER ONE
WATERSPOUT! . . . 4

CHAPTER TWO
THE SCIENCE BEHIND WATERSPOUTS . . . 10

CHAPTER THREE
WHERE TO SEE A WATERSPOUT . . . 16

Glossary . . . 22
Fast Facts . . . 23
One Stride Further . . . 23
Find Out More . . . 24
Index . . . 24

CHAPTER ONE
WATERSPOUT!

"Come and eat!" Mateo's sister Isabella called to him. He left the edge of the water and ran toward the picnic bench.

Mateo and his family were on vacation. They had driven down to the Florida Keys, a string of islands off the tip of the southern state. It was a warm, breezy day. Clouds dotted the sky above the deep, blue ocean.

Mateo brushed the sand off his legs and sat down on the bench, facing the water. He loved looking at the ocean. He hoped to see a big fish or a cool boat. As he scanned the water, he did see something! It looked like a dark, round spot on the water's surface. Maybe it was some kind of sea life coming up for air?

"What's that, Dad?" Mateo nudged his father and pointed to the dark circle. "Whoa! Now it looks different!"

A **column** had formed. It was tube shaped. It rose up from the water to the base of the cloud overhead. The column was spinning.

Fair-weather waterspouts start with swirling water on the surface.

Dad grabbed his cell phone. "I'll try to get a video," he told Mateo.

As Mateo watched, the spinning column slowed and faded. In a few minutes, it was gone.

Some waterspouts happen during thunderstorms. Others form in calm weather.

"That was a waterspout!" Isabella said. "We learned about them in science class. They're sort of like tornadoes over the water."

A tornado is one of the most violent forms of weather. Tornadoes are narrow, spinning columns of air that form between thunderstorms and the ground. They are made up of water droplets, dust, and **debris**. Waterspouts are similar. A waterspout is a spinning tube of air and water. When water and air spin around, they create a **vortex** on the surface of a body of water. This is similar to the **whirlpool** of spinning water that forms in a draining sink or bathtub. Waterspouts are made of mist from clouds. They can form over oceans and lakes. They usually form over warm ocean waters.

There are two types of waterspouts. Fair-weather waterspouts form in warm weather with light winds. This is the type Mateo saw. Fair-weather waterspouts start under cumulus (KYOO-myuh-lus) clouds. They move upward from the surface of the water toward the cloud. They usually form when a light wind blows in the morning or early afternoon. They do not move around much.

The second type is the tornadic waterspout. These are more dangerous than fair-weather waterspouts. Tornadic waterspouts are tornadoes that form over water. They can also start out as a tornado over land. If the tornado moves over water, it becomes a waterspout. Tornadic waterspouts typically form in the late afternoon or evening.

CUMULUS CLOUDS

Scientists group clouds into ten types. These groups are based on how high the clouds form in the sky. Cumulus clouds are in the low group. They are dense and bright white on top. They sometimes look like a head of cauliflower. They often have dark, flat bases.

Thunderstorms over water can form tornadic waterspouts.

They usually form during thunderstorms. They occur when there is warm, moist air and heavy winds. Tornadic waterspouts form downward, from top to bottom.

CHAPTER TWO

THE SCIENCE BEHIND WATERSPOUTS

There are major differences in how the two types of waterspouts form. But there are also similarities. Waterspouts form when warm, moist air meets cooler air higher in the **atmosphere**. These conditions make the air rotate, or spin.

Fair-weather waterspouts form between the surface of an ocean or lake and overhead cumulus clouds with flat bases. Clouds form when water vapor **condenses** into ice crystals or water droplets. Water vapor is invisible **moisture** in the air. It is water in the form of gas.

THE WATER CYCLE

Water is constantly moving through Earth and the atmosphere. This is called the water cycle. Liquid water **evaporates** and becomes water vapor. Water vapor condenses into clouds. Then rain and snow fall back to Earth. Water can also evaporate through plants. In addition, solid ice and snow can turn into gas.

Cumulonimbus (kyoo-myuh-loh-NIM-buss) clouds are the kind associated with thunderstorms.

Warm air can hold more moisture than cool air. As the air cools, the water vapor condenses. The gas changes to liquid water droplets or solid ice crystals. These water droplets make clouds visible.

Fair-weather spouts go through five stages. In the first stage, warm, moist, windy air rises from the water and pushes against the cool air above it. This makes the air spin around in a vortex. At the same time, water droplets that have condensed in the cumulus cloud move downward. The vortex is made up of spinning, rising air and moisture from the cloud above. A dark spot appears on the surface of the water where the base of the vortex touches it. In the second stage, the vortex spins against the surface of the water. Bands of water spin out in a **spiral** pattern on the water's surface. Third, a spray of water swirls up around the base of the vortex. In the fourth stage, the spinning column rises upward. This is when the waterspout is at its strongest. It stretches between the water and the cloud. In the last stage, the flow of warm air into the spout grows weaker. This causes the spray to spread out and disappear.

DARK SPOT

SPIRAL

Fair-weather waterspouts start with a dark spot on the water. As the vortex spins, water spirals out from the dark spot.

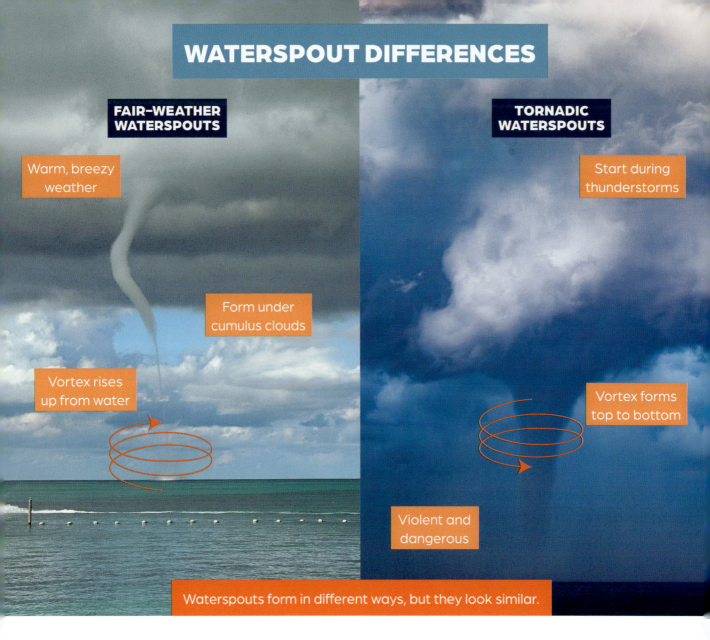

Waterspouts form in different ways, but they look similar.

Fair-weather waterspouts are more common but less violent than tornadic waterspouts. Fair-weather spouts do not move much. This makes them easier to avoid. They also rarely come onto land. If they do, they break up quickly.

Tornadic waterspouts can form over the water. But they can also form as tornadoes on land. Tornadoes come from thunderstorms. Thunderstorms form when warm, moist air rises and collides with cold air higher in the atmosphere. The warm air gets colder as it rises. This makes drops of water, which become a cumulus cloud. Then the cooled air falls back down, where it warms up again. The loop of warming and cooling air is called a convection cell. Some convection cells have rotating winds inside them. These cells can cause tornadoes.

If a tornado moves over the water, it becomes a tornadic waterspout. The opposite is true, too. If a tornadic waterspout moves onto land, the National Weather Service (NWS) issues a tornado warning. Fair-weather waterspouts mostly stay in the same spot. But tornadic waterspouts can move across the water. This is one of the reasons tornadic waterspouts are more dangerous. They are also stronger. Another danger comes from the thunderstorms in which they form. Storms often come with other dangerous weather, including hail, lightning, high winds, and heavy rain.

CHAPTER THREE

WHERE TO SEE A WATERSPOUT

Weather experts cannot predict the exact time or place a waterspout will occur. But they can identify the weather conditions that make waterspouts likely. They also know which locations often have waterspouts. A good source for waterspout forecast information is the National Oceanic and Atmospheric Administration (NOAA). The NWS also monitors waterspouts.

Waterspouts are spotted in the Florida Keys more than any other place in the world. The Florida Keys can have up to 500 waterspouts in a year. Tornadic waterspouts can occur there anytime of year. They usually form in the afternoon or evening, which is when thunderstorms are most likely to occur. Fair-weather waterspouts normally happen in the morning or early afternoon during the summer months.

To see a fair-weather waterspout, people can watch for a line of cumulus clouds with dark, flat bases on summer days with light wind.

On September 12, 2013, two waterspouts formed on Lake Michigan near Kenosha, Wisconsin.

Waterspouts are common in tropical areas such as the Philippines.

Waterspouts occur in other warm, **tropical** places as well. The Greek islands and the east coast of Australia are places waterspouts can form. Waterspouts form over the Gulf of Mexico, the Bahamas, and the Gulf Stream. Cienfuegos Bay in Cuba and the west coast of Africa are other areas where waterspouts are common.

Waterspouts are not limited to the tropics. They can be seen in the Great Lakes in North America. These usually form in August, September, and October, when the lake waters are warmest. Cold air moves across the lakes as the season changes. This creates good conditions for waterspout formation. Waterspouts have also been spotted near Seattle, Washington, and the Grand Banks of Newfoundland, Canada. People have also seen waterspouts off the coasts of China and Japan.

HOW BIG AND FAST?

Waterspouts can range from a few feet wide to more than 300 feet (90 m) wide. Wind speeds average 50 miles per hour (80 kph). This is equal to a weak land tornado. Waterspouts usually last for 5 to 10 minutes. Some large waterspouts can last for an hour.

Like tornadoes, waterspouts can be dangerous. Tornadic waterspouts can move toward land. If people see one, they should take cover or **evacuate**. Boats or swimmers should steer away from a waterspout, traveling away at a 90-degree angle to the waterspout's path. They should not move closer to get a better look. NOAA Weather Radio sends out warnings when weather conditions are right for waterspouts. Boaters can stay informed by listening. People in or near the water can also look for dark, flat-bottomed cumulus clouds, storm conditions, and wind. By being careful, those lucky enough to see an amazing waterspout can enjoy this natural **phenomenon** while staying safe.

Waterspouts can be dangerous to boats.

GLOSSARY

atmosphere (AT-muss-feer) An atmosphere is the layer of gases that surrounds a planet. Clouds form in Earth's atmosphere.

column (KAH-lum) A column is an upright tube or cylinder. A waterspout is a column of spinning air and water.

condenses (kun-DENSS-iz) When a substance condenses, it changes from vapor or gas to liquid. Moisture in clouds condenses from water vapor to liquid water.

debris (duh-BREE) Debris is made up of pieces of things that have been destroyed or broken down. Tornadoes are made of water droplets, debris, and dust.

evacuate (eh-VAK-yoo-ayt) To evacuate means to leave a place where one might be in danger. People should evacuate if they see a tornadic waterspout.

evaporates (ih-VA-puh-raytz) When something evaporates, it transforms from liquid to vapor. Liquid water evaporates into water vapor, then it condenses into clouds.

moisture (MOYSS-chur) Moisture is a small amount of liquid that causes dampness. Condensation in clouds causes moisture in the air.

phenomenon (fuh-NAH-muh-nahn) A phenomenon is an observable event that can be explained by science. Waterspouts are a natural phenomenon.

spiral (SPY-ruhl) A spiral is a shape that spins around a center point. Waterspouts create a spiral on the water's surface.

tropical (TRAW-pih-kull) A tropical climate is one where temperatures usually do not dip below freezing. Waterspouts are common in tropical places.

vortex (VOHR-teks) A vortex is a spinning mass of water or moist air. A waterspout forms a vortex above the water.

whirlpool (WURL-pool) A whirlpool is water spinning in a spiral. Water draining from a bathtub forms a whirlpool.

FAST FACTS

✹ Waterspouts are spinning columns of air and moisture. They are similar to tornadoes, but they occur over water instead of land.

✹ Fair-weather waterspouts occur under cumulus clouds in mild weather. They are more common than tornadic waterspouts.

✹ Tornadic waterspouts can start on land and move to water, or they can start over water. They occur during thunderstorms.

✹ Fair-weather waterspouts are less violent and dangerous than tornadic waterspouts.

✹ The Florida Keys experience up to 500 waterspouts per year. Waterspouts can also occur over the Great Lakes.

ONE STRIDE FURTHER

✹ Think about the weather and the geography where you live. Is there a chance you might see a waterspout near your home? Why or why not?

✹ The National Oceanic and Atmospheric Administration (NOAA) and the National Weather Service (NWS) are both government agencies that collect and report information about waterspouts. How is this helpful to people? What kinds of workers might need this information?

✹ Imagine you are at the beach and you see what you think is a tornadic waterspout over the water. What would you do?

FIND OUT MORE

IN THE LIBRARY

Barber, Nichola. *Eyewitness Workbooks: Weather*.
New York, NY: DK Publishing, 2020.

Cappucci, Matthew. *Extreme Weather for Kids*. Beverly, MA: Quarry Books, 2024.

Kentner, Julie. *Thunderstorms*. Parker, CO: The Child's World, 2025.

ON THE WEB

Visit our website for links about waterspouts:

childsworld.com/links

Note to Parents, Caregivers, Teachers, and Librarians: We routinely verify our web links to make sure they are safe and active sites. So encourage your readers to check them out!

INDEX

boats, 4, 20

condensation, 10–12
cumulus clouds, 8, 10, 12, 14, 15, 17, 20

fair-weather waterspouts, 4–8, 10, 12–15, 16–17
Florida Keys, 4, 16

Great Lakes, 19

how waterspouts form, 4–7, 8–9, 10–15

lakes, 7, 10, 19

NOAA, 16, 20
NWS, 15, 16

oceans, 4–7, 10, 18–19

safety, 8, 14, 15, 20
size, 19

thunderstorms, 7, 9, 14, 15, 16, 20
tornadic waterspouts, 8–9, 14–15, 16, 20
tornadoes, 7–8, 15, 19, 20

vapor, 10–11
vortexes, 7, 12, 14

water cycle, 10